YOU ARE
GOD'S
MASTERPIECE

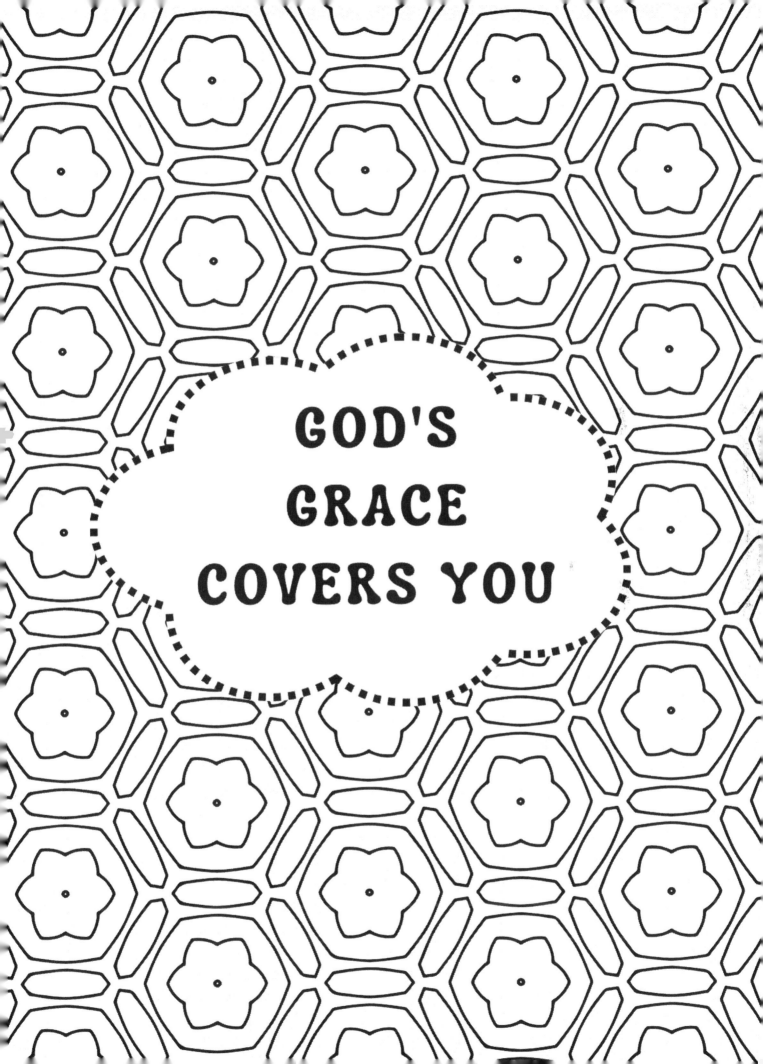

KEEP YOUR HEART CENTERED ON CHRIST

GOD
IS
NEAR

YOUR FAITH JOURNEY IS A MASTERPIECE, COLORED BY GOD'S GRACE

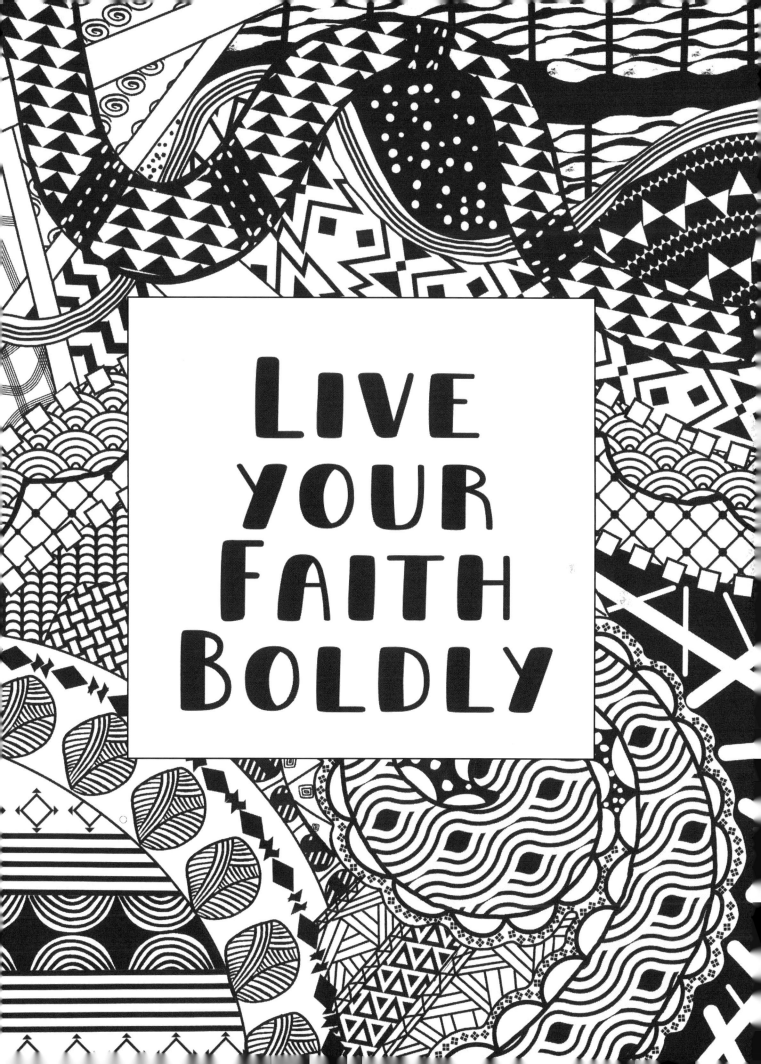

you have been
uniquely
designed for a
purpose

HE NEVER GIVES UP ON YOU

You have
an unique
calling

YOUR FAITH SHINES LIKE A STAR

LET HIS
LOVE FILL
YOUR HEART

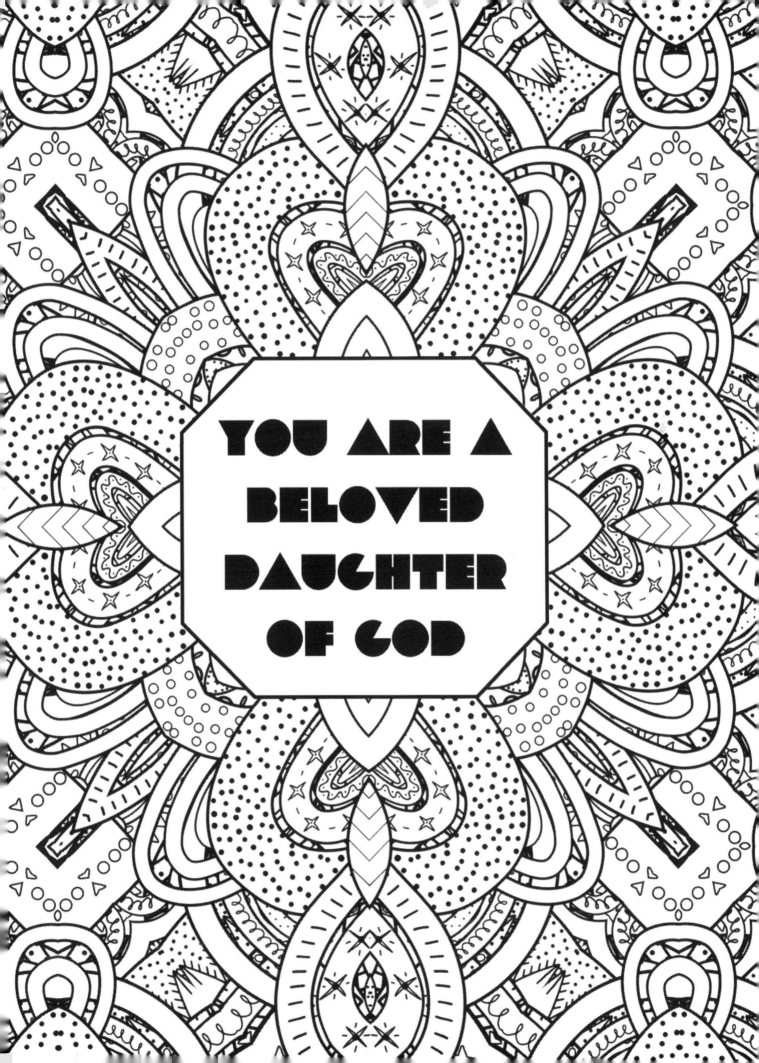

HEAVEN SMILES ON YOU

LOVE GOD
LOVE OTHERS
LOVE YOU

GOD HAD YOU IN MIND BEFORE YOU WERE BORN

LET YOUR LIGHT SPARKLE FOR JESUS

YOU CAN
DO HARD
THINGS

CHOSEN AND LOVED BY THE CREATOR

You are precious to God

Made in the USA
Columbia, SC
05 September 2023